MW01106867

THE BOOK OF POSITIVITY, MOTIVATION, & SUCCESS

WISE
WORDS
from
WISE
PEOPLE

SHAWN M. ROGERS

Charleston, SC
www.PalmettoPublishing.com

Wise Words from Wise People
Copyright © 2021 by Shawn M. Rogers

First Edition

Hardcover ISBN: 978-1-68515-034-1
Paperback ISBN: 978-1-68515-035-8

PREFACE

In search of my passion. In search of what motivates me, I used almost the entire year of 2020 journaling my thoughts. From various outlets, anything I felt could be used to my advantage was written down.

I let a few friends hold on to my personal journals after they were filled top to bottom, front to back and the feedback received gave me a "lightbulb" moment; I'm going to get this published. If I could motivate them and provide an inspirational tool for them to pull from, why not make my thoughts a reality? From that very moment on, doing this became a goal of mine I had to get accomplished.

I'm not going to take the credit for the gems and knowledge given within this book, as I'm still learning and applying those to my personal life, but I will take credit for breaking down my interpretation. Breaking down and paraphrasing these highly acclimated individuals. Each and every one of them lived their own stories and had their own spin on how they motivate.

Use this book as a tool. Use it to motivate yourself. We all have individual reasons that fuel us, and this book is the gas to an empty tank.

I am no motivational speaker, but I'm someone speaking from experience. The highs and lows of life. What motivates me. ..... who doesn't need an extra dose of motivation from time to time? A spark.

Motivation from my perspective… even if I can motivate and inspire just one person, my mission would be fulfilled …. if one person comes across my book on an outlet platform, or hand to hand delivery and it gives them that extra boost of motivation "job well done" … "I'd give myself a literal and figurative pat on the back….

I'm just your average guy chasing my full potential in hopes to provide the best life possible for myself and my family…I'm just the messenger and hope you enjoy.

INTRODUCTION

Finding ways to motivate ourselves, can at times, become draining. Having a resource right at your fingertips is the main goal to the audience interested in giving this a read. Pick a page, any page and that message may be exactly what you have been looking for.

In most situations, you have to read through books and highlight the key points/ gems you find… in this interactive journal simplicity is key; every single page is worth the read. There are gems and takeaways from every page within… that's the value being provided.

I wanted to make this more of an interactive journal, than your standard book. The idea behind what has been provided is meant to be indefinite. This is pageless and never ending. Every single time you open this book, will be like your first time again. Each page is dedicated to motivating the reader for the day and give them that extra push to chase their dreams. Unlocking their full potential. Throughout reading, which I recommend 4-5 pages at a time, you can also write your own ideas, thoughts, goals, etc.

The goal isn't to knock out every page and complete this reading in entirety within one day… Pinpoint times where you're feeling down. Times when you don't have the energy to get up and work for what you deserve. When you need that extra push of motivation, you open up any random page and you'll come across something that'll completely shift your current state of thinking. If you happen to be an individual who is "always" motivated by yourself, even better. This will just add fuel to that fire.

There has also been provided designated spaces in between the messages for the reader to place their input. Reflect how they feel and connect with whatever it is they just read. Toward the end of the journal, there are full page sections that are blank canvases to just write whatever it is you so please. You must write down anything that you want to accomplish, so that you can check it off when it's met. You must speak your wants and wishes into the universe.

"Speak it into existence, give it time, and watch the magic you can create."

Write yourself a blank check...
Imagine going to the bank and cashing it.

		1027

DATE _____

PAY TO THE
ORDER OF _____ $ _____

_____ DOLLARS

Security
Features
Details on
Back

FOR _____

⑆ 2 2 2 2 2 2 2 2 ⑆ 000 ⑈ 111 555 ⑈ 1027

Practice your signature. It will be worth millions one day.

X _____

X _____

X _____

X _____

X _____

X _____

TOP 5 WORDS TO KEEP IN MIND WHILE READING...

1. **Mindset**—#1 key to unlocking your full potential. It starts here. The first change that must take place is in your mind. You have to adjust your mind and your thinking, before you change your way of living. Start here...

2. **Motivation**—Internally, or externally, we must search and find what drives us. What lights our fire within? We all have it, we just need to unlock it!

3. **Inspiration**—I never would've thought I'd have a professionally published journal on all major platforms. This recently became a goal of mine and it is now checked off my bucket list. You can do whatever you put your mind to. Take action. There is no time like now. Tomorrow is never promised.

4. **Success**—What does it REALLY take to reach the level of success you set for yourself? It won't be easy. We all have our own meanings and definitions, as well as different paths to becoming successful. We owe it to ourselves to be the best we can be. Are you living, or are you just surviving?

5. **Legacy**—This is what we do it for. Leaving a positive impact and setting your mark on the world that will last long after your time passes. Do it for yourself. Do it for your family. Do it for your LEGACY.

What motivates you?

_____

_____

_____

_____

_____

_____

What is your definition of Success?

_____

_____

_____

_____

_____

_____

What is your definition of Legacy?

_____

_____

_____

_____

_____

_____

List of Books to Read:

"Over the years, I have personally read, or am in the process of reading these highly recommended books below. Finding gems and keys of the successful, or just those you look up to are always within books. You just have to look for them." Seek and you shall find...

- Think and Grow Rich

- The Power of Positive Thinking

- The Power of Habit

- The Power of Your Subconscious Mind

- The Magic of Thinking BIG

- Contagious

- The Richest Man in Babylon

- Rich Dad, Poor Dad

- The Millionaire Next Door

- 48 Laws of Power

And last, but not least, the main influence behind me taking action on creating this interactive journal:

—The Gucci Mane Guide to Greatness

"Just like most things in life… it requires time to grow. As we continue growing and strengthening ourselves, we can one day reach our full potential…continue to water your mind, water your mindset, have patience and our full forms will begin to blossom"

"One seed at a time"

#1 KEY

"The first change that needs to take place is in your mind... You have to change your mind, before you change the way you're living. The way you move..."

"CONQUER THE DAY"

"THE WORLD IS YOURS"

NO RUSH

PROGRESSION
DIRECTION
HAPPINESS
WEALTH
BALANCE

Less is More

"Eliminate all distractions"

"TUNNEL VISION"

What's most important to you?

_____

_____

_____

_____

_____

_____

_____

_____

_____

_____

_____

_____

_____

_____

"Day by Day, Brick by Brick"

"Every day is a BLESSING"

THE PROCESS
"You must go through it"

HIGHS
LOWS,
GOOD
BAD

"Who do you want to become"

"New Day, New Opportunities"

WORDS OF THE DAY:

GO

CAPITALIZE

FOCUS

BRAINSTORM

STRATEGY

GAMEPLAN

EXECUTE

CONFIDENCE

HUMBLE

"Think outside the box"

5 P's

Proper
Preparation
Prevents
Poor
Performance

"Stay ready, so you don't have to get ready"

If an opportunity you have been waiting for presents itself, are you ready to do what it takes? Are you up for the task? When this moment approaches, there is nothing better than having that *"I've been waiting for this my whole life"* approach. I'm ready, are you?

CHERISH EVERY SINGLE DAY

"Life is so valuable… here one day and gone the next."

*Make **EVERYDAY** count.*
Live life to the fullest.

MAKE A DIFFERENCE.

LEAVE YOUR MARK.

"What's your PURPOSE?"

_____

_____

_____

_____

_____

WORDS OF THE DAY:

LOVE
LIVE
LIFE
HOPE
DREAM
WISH
HAPPINESS
PRAY

LIFE IS ABOUT CHOICES:

"Chances you take, Choices you make..."

"Think of all the chances you did, or didn't take and ask yourself, would you be in a different position?"

"What about the choices you have made. One good, or one bad choice can determine the next steps in your life"

GO HARD
BELIEVE IN YOURSELF

"Stick to the Script"

VISION

_____

_____

_____

GOALS

_____

_____

_____

CONFIDENCE IS KEY

"Lift whatever it is on your back and carry the weight"

"Rome wasn't built in a day…"

WORDS OF THE DAY:

LEARN
GROW
EVOLVE
POTENTIAL
EXPERIENCES
LESSON
OVERCOME

"Don't underestimate the GREATNESS inside of you"

"YOU create your own DESTINY"

"Stumble into Success"

Things do not always go as planned...

KEEP GIVING EFFORT

IMAGINE WHAT COULD BE

Imagine a tree:
Imagine a table...
Imagine a fancy chair...
Imagine a log cabin...
Now realize what it started as...
"We have the tools and resources right in front of us... we just have to figure out how to make use of them"

Imagine
Imagination

"SUCCESS IS LIKE AN ICEBERG..."

WHAT THEY SEE:

SUCCESS
MONEY
GLORY
REWARDS
MATERIAL ITEMS

WHAT THEY DON'T SEE:
GRIND
FAILURE
HARD-WORK
STRUGGLE
SACRIFICE
LONG NIGHTS
EARLY MORNINGS

"Are you prepared to do what it takes to be Successful?"

"DON'T TALK ABOUT IT, BE ABOUT IT"

ACTIONS!
ACTIONS!
ACTIONS!

"TURN A NEGATIVE, INTO A POSITIVE"

HAVE A PLAN

"Sharpen your skills"

"Strategize"

WORDS OF THE DAY

REFLECTION:

- *Short term GOALS-*
- *Long term GOALS-*
- *ACCOMPLISHMENTS-*

"What adjustments need to be made?"

_____

_____

_____

GOALS:

- *Career?*

_____

_____

_____

- *Where do I want to be in 5 years?*

_____

_____

_____

"MILLIONAIRE WHO RETIRED AT 36"

6 PRINCIPLES TO LIVE BY:

1. *Make financial freedom your #1 GOAL*

2. *Actively boost your Income*

3. *Invest in appreciating assets*

4. *Automate, automate, automate*

5. *Know where your money is going*

6. *Detach yourself from things you don't need*

"Do you want to be financially free"

WORDS OF THE DAY:

FINANCIAL FREEDOM
OWNERSHIP
INVESTING
CREDIT
ASSETS
EQUITY
PROPERTY
REAL ESTATE
WEALTH
RETIREMENT

"Increase your financial knowledge
if you want to reach financial freedom"

"If you want it, you can get it"

MAKE IT HAPPEN

NO HANDOUTS

"Be fearless when you wake up"

ACTIONS> WORDS

"Are you taking action, or just talking about it?

"Don't downgrade your DREAMS to match your reality, UPGRADE your FAITH to match your VISION"

"Challenges are what make LIFE interesting. Overcoming them is what makes life meaningful"

TAKE RISK

"Old keys can't unlock NEW DOORS"

RE- CHARGE YOUR PASSION
RE- CHARGE YOUR VISION
RE- CHARGE YOUR PURPOSE

"MIND OVER MATTER"

MENTALITY

STRONG
POSITIVE
WINNER

"I WILL NOT LOSE"

"MAMBA MENTALITY"

"YOU ARE YOUR ONLY COMPETITION"

"DON'T LET EXCUSES BE THE REASON YOU COME UP SHORT IN LIFE"

NEW DAY

NEW MONTH

NEW OPPORTUNITIES

WORD OF
THE DAY:

CAPITALIZE!

"TURN YOUR DREAMS INTO REALITY"

"KNOWLEDGE IS POWER!"

MAJOR KEY ALERT:

- ## KEEP LEARNING
- ## EDUCATE YOURSELF
- ## READ/RESEARCH

FEED YOUR BRAIN

"Direction is way more important than speed"

"Make it a goal of yours to learn something new every day"

NOBODY CARES WORK HARDER

Point, blank, period...

There are 3 types of people in this world:

1. GRINDERS—FIND A WAY!
2. COMPLAINERS
3. HATERS

"WHICH ONE ARE YOU?"

"If you aren't a grinder, you have to switch that up ASAP"

GOALS...
DREAMS...
WISHES...

*"You can have it all, but you have to **PUT THE WORK IN**"*

"Hard-work PAYS OFF"

"PERFECT DAY TO BOSS UP"

KEEP LEARNING

KEEP GROWING

VISUALIZE

THOUGHTS

"Don't take NO for an answer"

"HAVE YOUR PLAN"

"STICK TO THE SCRIPT"

"Commitment separates those who live their DREAMS, from those who live their lives with regret of missed OPPORTUNITIES"

What separates the <u>GOOD</u> from the <u>EXCEPTIONAL?</u>

VISION

INNOVATIVE THINKING

CONSISTENCY

EXECUTION

"Do you want to be good, or exceptional?"

NEVER STOP, NEVER SETTLE

"FALL DOWN 7 TIMES, GET UP 8"

*"THE ONLY PLACE **SUCCESS** COMES BEFORE **HARD-WORK** IS THE DICTIONARY"*

KEEP PUSHING
KEEP GRINDING
STAY FOCUSED

"THE MARATHON CONTINUES"

NEW DAY, NEW OPPORTUNITIES

ACCOUNTABILITY!

SACRIFICE!

"Change your attitude"

EXECUTE
EXECUTE
EXECUTE

QUESTION OF THE DAY:

What are you willing to do, to reach your GOALS?

_____

_____

_____

_____

What are you willing to do, to be SUCCESSFUL?

_____

_____

_____

_____

"Do you have what it takes?"

_____

_____

_____

_____

"Take control of your OWN LIFE"

"Chess NOT checkers"

Monday, get better….

Tuesday, get better….

"Get better every single day and as days, weeks, months, years pass, you'll look in the mirror at the very person you wanted to become."

*"Show up for yourself every day. Your **<u>REALITY</u>** is a reflection of your **<u>WORK ETHIC</u>"***

GRIND

GRIND

GRIND

*"Change your **<u>MINDSET</u>**, change your **<u>LIFE</u>"***

"FOCUS IN"

"Step outside of your
COMFORT ZONE"

WORDS OF THE DAY:

RISK

ELEVATE

LEVEL UP

"What do you want out of LIFE?"

"Accept the unknown..."

*"At the end of the day, people are going to judge you anyway. DON'T LIVE up to their expectations, **LIVE UP TO YOURS!**"*

*"Don't try and impress other people, **IMPRESS YOURSELF**"*

*"Don't let other people set goals for yourself, **SET YOUR OWN**"*

"GO out there and GET IT"

NO RISK!
NO REWARD!

What are you willing to do, to make it happen?

WORDS OF THE DAY:

EXECUTE
HUSTLE
MANIFEST
MENTALITY
GRIND
CAPITALIZE
SUCCESS

"FOCUS ON YOUR JOURNEY"

NO RUSH

PATIENCE

ELIMINATE DISTRACTIONS

YOUR JOURNEY

YOUR TIME WILL COME

"Continue watering your seeds"

"Let them grow. Let them blossom"

"Set yourself up for the best future possible"
(MARATHON MENTALITY)

WORDS OF THE DAY:

INVEST
LONGEVITY
STOCKS
BONDS
ETF'S
INDEX FUNDS
IRA'S
BROKERAGE
LEGACY

"ARE YOU SET UP FOR FINANCIAL SUCCESS?"

MENTAL TOUGHNESS
"Believe in yourself…"

MENTALITY
OVERCOME
BATTLE
WAR!

"Patience is a Virtue"

"What are you willing to go through?"

DAMON DASH INTERVIEW POINTS:

- Residual Income

- Independence

- Prepare for the moment (good, or bad)

- Financial empowerment

- Have / get information and APPLY IT

- Everything is a learning experience

- SOLUTIONS > PROBLEMS

- Celebrate the process/ progress

"If they can do it, I CAN DO IT"

WHAT IS THE 50/ 30/ 20 BUDGET RULE?

50% NEEDS

30% WANTS

20% SAVING

Money management is **KEY**

"NO BAD DEBTS"

"ASSETS > LIABILITIES"

"Education
Before
Compensation"

"You can't skip steps…"

"YOU HAVE TO PAY YOUR
DUES"

"Stop lining your life up with
BILLS and start lining your
*life up with **PURPOSE***"

"FIND YOUR PURPOSE"

*"Your **MIND** must reach the destination before your **BODY** does…"*

Be MENTALLY prepared for the JOURNEY

UPS & DOWNS NEVER QUIT...

"Embrace failure"

*"Get **YOUR MIND** right"*

WORD OF THE DAY:

FAILURE

Failure is a MASSIVE part of SUCCESS

Failure is where ALL the lessons are!

CONTROLLED FAILURE:

EVOLVE
GROW

"Are you prepared to fail?

"Do you welcome failure?"

"Become comfortable, being uncomfortable"

*"Your **perspective** on LIFE will determine your DESTINATION"*

*"If you can't change the situation, change the **PERSPECTIVE**"*

*"You become what you **PRIORITIZE**"*

"Do you have your priorities in order?"

"5 Valuable Money Lessons you can learn from Monopoly"

1. Don't sit on too much cash

2. Avoid spending all your money right away

3. Diversify your Portfolio

4. Learn how to negotiate

5. Be patient—play the long game

VALUE
LESSONS
LEARN

"Who would've thought we were learning lifelong lessons playing board games in our youth? The keys are always around us, we just have to be aware"

"You CANNOT win against the world, if you CANNOT win the WAR against your MIND"

SELF- DISCIPLINE is the **KEY**

PRIORITIES

"Remove CAN'T from your Vocabulary"

"If you want it, what are you waiting for?"

YOUR <u>MINDSET</u> IS YOUR REALITY!

"When patience meets consistency, you get POSITIVE RESULTS"

KOBE BRYANT'S 10 RULES OF SUCCESS:

1. Follow your passion

2. Find mentors

3. Don't fear failure

4. Have patience

5. Learn from failures

6. Focus on winning

7. Love what you do

8. Elevate others

9. Protect your dreams

10. Learn from the best/ STUDY!

REST IN PEACE 8/24

"Life isn't waiting for ANYBODY"

No matter what's going on, LIFE IS STILL HAPPENING…

SNAP OUT OF IT!

YOU HAVE TO GO!

NEVER GIVE UP!

STOP PLAYING AROUND!

"PUT YOUR PLANS IN MOTION"

**EXECUTE
EXECUTION**

"MAKE SOMETHING
OUT OF NOTHING"

NO EXCUSES

*"You either want it, or you
don't, but the choice is yours"*

"Cost of Hesitation"

YOU BREAK THE RYTHEM

YOU LOSE MOMEMTUM

"You break your rhythm and what would've flowed, is now off sync…"

"If not now, then when?"

"Don't miss your chance…your turn"

Avoid unintended consequences… you may never get the same opportunity…

MOVEMENT

"When your opportunity presents itself, MAKE YOUR MOVE"

*"YOU MISS **100%** of the shots YOU DON'T TAKE"*

WORK FOR IT!
TAKE IT!
NO HAND OUTS!
NO EASY ROUTES!

"Are you a WOLF, or a SHEEP?"

"BE A DOG!"

QUESTIONS OF THE DAY:

What are you willing to **SACRIFICE**???

_____

_____

_____

What are you willing to do to achieve your **GOALS**???

_____

_____

_____

START NOW...

GET SERIOUS...

"VISUALIZE SUCCESS"

Work before celebration…
Put your WORK IN

Take YOUR LIFE to
the NEXT LEVEL

WORK
WORK
WORK

LEVEL UP

"You are going to get **<u>TESTED</u>** *in life…"*

STAY DOWN
DISCIPLINE
BELIEVE (YOU WILL)

"Do you **REALLY BELIEVE** *in the* **DREAM** *you have for yourself?"*

"Believe in Yourself
and who you want to become"

"Don't be afraid of the
<u>CHALLENGES</u> *that come with*
living the life you want to LIVE"

Welcome challenges…
Embrace challenges…

CHALLENGE YOURSELF

"Embrace the STRUGGLE"

"You can either let tough times
MAKE YOU, or BREAK YOU"

*"Make something happen
for yourself…"*

**MATERIALIZE
MANIFEST**

Time/ Energy
Give/ Take

Not about what you say, it's about
WHAT YOU DO…

STOP PLAYING WITH TIME…

THE TIME IS NOW!

*"The strongest factor for **SUCCESS** is **SELF-ESTEEM**"*

*Believing you **CAN** do it…*

*Believing you **DESERVE** it…*

*Believing you **WILL** be successful…*

NO LIMITS

NO MATTER WHAT

STAY FOCUSED

"STAY DOWN FOR WHAT YOU BELIEVE IN"

"Don't fall victim to the distractions that come with your journey of trying to get to SUCCESS"

YOUR JOURNEY

TUNNEL VISION

"Eliminate ALL distractions"

"Focus only on YOUR GOALS"

"ESCAPE THE BRAINWASH"

UN LEARN
RE LEARN

Get rid of the **AVERAGE**
MINDSET

DIVE IN HEADFIRST…

Don't be afraid of the deep end!

"Get rid of that security blanket that's keeping you comfortable"

JUMP. GO. NOW.

"You become what you **CONSTANTLY** *think about…"*

The **<u>POWER</u>** *of the mind…*

THOUGHTS

"Thinking about **<u>SUCCESS</u>** isn't enough to make it happen. You also have to take **<u>ACTION</u>!**"

Thoughts- Actions- Repeat

4 Millionaire **HABITS** that
WILL CHANGE YOUR LIFE...

1. Producing vs. consuming

    •   Shift the way you use/ spend your time
    •   We all have the same 24 hours
    •   Move your financial needle

2. Don't make excuses

    •   DON'T BE FEARFUL—take action
    •   The way you get past fear and excuses is taking action
    •   JUST DO IT

3. NETWORKING

    •   IRON SHARPENS IRON
    •   Be influenced- STUDY
    •   Re shape your MIND/ THINKING

4. HAVE FUN!

    •   ENJOY YOUR JOURNEY
    •   ENJOY YOUR PROCESS

BLUEPRINT TO SUCCESS:

DREAM *"If you can dream it & VISUALIZE it, then you can REALIZE IT"*

PREPARATION

- *Education = LEARNING*
- *Mentorship*
- *PLAN, PLAN, PLAN*

HARD-WORK

- *Working toward goals…*
- *Working toward becoming better overall…*
- *NO DAYS OFF*
- *GRIND*

*"There is **NO** end when it comes to **UNDERSTANDING, KNOWLEDGE, LEARNING, GROWTH, EDUCATION, TRAINING, and SHARPENING YOUR SKILLS"***

"Each of us has a unique genius inside waiting to express itself for the benefit of others; it's an asset waiting to be discovered, enhanced, and made even more valuable…"

What are you bringing to the table?

_____

_____

_____

_____

_____

WARREN BUFFET 6 PIECES OF WISDOM:

1. Think LONG-TERM

2. Stay the course

3. Marry the right person

4. Invest, invest, invest

5. INVEST IN YOURSELF- KEY

6. Money isn't everything

    - Family
    - Values
    - Morals

"Learn from those who are successful. Soak up as much knowledge as possible. Apply that knowledge to the best of your abilities"

"PRESSURE MAKES DIAMONDS"

What are you capable of?

Do you have what it takes?

When your back is up against the wall, what's your next move?

BOSS MENTALITY

"It costs to be the BOSS, remember that"

"At some point, you don't need any more advice, motivational quotes, or clever sayings… You just need silence, determination, & work ethic…"

HARD WORK= RESULTS

"Stay down, until you come up"

"NOTHING GREAT IN LIFE WILL EVER COME EASY"

The ups & downs during your journey are simply a continuous TEST to see if you REALLY want what you are seeking in LIFE...

"Learn from the rainy days, don't live in them"

YOUR MIND is *POWERFUL*

YOUR MIND is the MASTER KEY!

*"You want to **GROW**, you got to **GO**"*

WATER your GROWTH
WATER your MINDSET

INSPIRATION
MOTIVATION

THINK BIGGER

DREAM BIGGER

"Moving away from your hometown is like the cheat code to life"

"New Experiences. New Points of View. New Perspectives"

"Success does not come from what you do occasionally. It comes from what you do **CONSISTENTLY**"

"CONSISTENCY IS KEY"

Work on your IDEAS
Work on your PLANS

KEEP PREPARING
KEEP LEARNING

"What ideas do you have in the works?"

_____

_____

_____

_____

_____

_____

_____

WORDS OF THE DAY:

GO
ACCOUNTABILITY
FOCUS
PRIORITIES
TIME- MANAGEMENT
WILLINGNESS
MASTERMIND
DETERMINATION
MAXIMIZE
EXECUTE
POSITIVITY

"Take a few moments and really break down what these words mean to you and why they are each important when reaching the level of success, we set for ourselves"

*"Change your **MINDSET**,
Change your **LIFE**"*

You are what you **THINK**

You are what you **BELIEVE**

MINDSET

"What you think about, you bring about"

SPEAK IT INTO EXISTENCE

***RESULTS
POSITIVITY***

"You are the average of the people you hang around"

SUCCESS NUTRITION FACTS:

Serving size: 24 hours a Day
Servings per container: 365 Days a
Year

Amount per serving:

Hustle	100%
Focus	100%
Persistence	100%
Discipline	100%
Failure	100%
Risk	100%
Patience	100%

***Percentages vary based on level of **AMBITION**

***Person above is ALL THE WAY FOCUSED IN

"Lazy is a disease"

DEVOURER SOMETHING EVERYDAY...

"A man is as he thinkith"

"We become what we think...what we say to ourselves...what we say out loud..."

"You will never know what you can be, or what you can do, until you GO ALL IN..."

Exhaust every option... then exhaust more

"Your miracles are never in what you've lost...it is always in what you have left..."

MASTER P'S 10 RULES FOR SUCCESS:

1. Have an entrepreneurial mindset

2. Stand by your word

3. Be prepared

4. Be independent

5. NETWORK

6. Create opportunities for yourself

7. Know your worth

8. Take chances on yourself

9. Makeup for your losses

10. Make history

"NO LIMIT"

"3 Simple Rules in Life…"

1. If you don't go after what you want, you will NEVER have it…

2. If you don't ask, the answer will ALWAYS be no…

3. If you don't step forward, you will ALWAYS be in the same place…

QUESTIONS TO ASK YOURSELF

Are you a fighter?

Are you a winner?

Are you UP FOR THE CHALLENGES?

Are you ready to GIVE IT YOUR ALL?

"*A wise man once said, don't be afraid to start over again. This time you're not starting from scratch, you're starting from* **EXPERIENCE**"

"Learn from the NEGATIVES"

"Turn losses into LESSONS"

FAITH= *seeing what's not yet there...you must believe that one day, you will see exactly what it is your looking for...*

CARPE DIEM=
SEIZE THE DAY

Take advantage of your 24 Hours

CAPITALIZE
EXECUTE

Daily Goals…
Weekly Goals…
Monthly Goals…
Yearly Goals…

"What are your upcoming goals (daily/ weekly/ monthly/ yearly) Give your-self a guide to revisit after months, or even years to see if you were able to meet them. What may need to change?"

*"No matter where you're at in **LIFE**, as long as you're breathing, you have a chance to be a **WINNER**"*

"BE A WINNER"

"Whatever you want to be, you can be"

THE WORLD IS **YOURS**...

THE FUTURE IS **YOURS**...

THE BUSINESS IS **YOURS**...

THE BAG IS **YOURS**...

"Remove CAN'T from your VOCABULARY"

"Be OBSESSED, or be AVERAGE"

Your path to happiness runs through your **OBSESSIONS**

Be OBSESSED with improvements…

Be OBSESSED with learning…

Obsession—"the domination of one's thoughts, or feelings by a persistent idea, image, desire, etc."

"What are your obsessions?"

_____

_____

_____

_____

_____

_____

*"Everything you need to **SUCCEED**, is right at your fingertips"*

NO EXCUSES

- YouTube University
- Books/ Articles
- INTERNET! GOOGLE!

DO YOUR RESEARCH
EDUCATE YOURSELF
GO FIND THE ANSWERS...

KNOWLEDGE IS POWER

NEVER STOP LEARNING

2 TYPES OF INDIVIDUALS:

1. The "Put me on" Mentality

vs.

2. The "I'll put myself on" Mentality

PUT THE WORK IN!
GRIND FOR YOURS!

"Nobody owes you anything. Stop feeling entitled. You have WORK FOR THIS! Let your work do the talking."

"Are you putting the work in?"

Are you grinding for everything you want?"

PAGE OF P'S:

PERSPECTIVE
PURPOSE
PREPARATION
POWER
PATIENCE
POSITIVITY
PRODUCTIVITY
POINT OF VIEW
PASSION

5 P'S:
PROPER
PLANNING
PREVENTS
POOR
PERFORMANCE

"He who fails to plan, plans to fail"

FAITH > FEAR

FEAR: What if I fail???

FAITH: What if I soar???

BELIEVE IN YOURSELF

"The riskiest thing you can do in LIFE, is take NO RISK!"

"You'll never get a hit from the dugout"

*MEASURED RISK
CALCULATED RISK*

NO RISK= NO REWARD!

"Take responsibility of your own LIFE"

It's NOT anybody's job to bail you out!

Stand on YOUR DECISIONS

TAKE ACCOUNTABILITY

NEWS FLASH NOBODY'S GOING TO BAIL YOU OUT WHEN YOU'RE GROWN

*TAKE CARE OF YOUR **RESPONSIBILITIES** IN LIFE...*

"THE WINNERS LIFESTYLE"

*"You have to let people, places, and things **GO** in order to **GROW**"*

*Ask yourself, what are you willing to let GO in order to **MATERIALIZE** your DREAMS???*

TIME
ENERGY

"What are you willing to give up?"

SACRIFICE
DISCIPLINE
CONSISTENCY

"Have FAITH"
"Fall in LOVE with the work"
"Maximize your potential"

3 Bones to live by:

1. **Wishbone**—Hoping and Praying

   - Hope = Motivator
   - Dream= The Driver

2. **Jawbone**—Courage to speak

   - TRUTH/ the power to lift your voice
   - SPEAK YOUR PURPOSE

3. **Backbone**—Courage to stand

   - STAND UP FOR YOURSELF
   - STAND UP FOR WHAT YOU BELIEVE IN

EXECUTION OVER EXCUSES

EXECUTION: THE CARRYING OUT, OR PUTTING INTO EFFECT OF A PLAN, ORDER, OR COURSE OF ACTION.

DAILY, MONTHLY, YEARLY=
GET BETTER

"DON'T LET FEAR BECOME A ROADBLOCK"

"THE DICTIONARY IS THE ONLY PLACE THAT SUCCESS COMES BEFORE WORK"

"THE WORK IS HOW YOU GET PUT ON!"

"WHEN YOU PUT THE WORK IN, YOU WILL GET THE RESULTS"

JAY Z'S 10 RULES OF SUCCESS:

1. Be the best

2. Make your own success

3. Take a chance

4. Have confidence

5. Learn from your failures

6. Avoid engaging egos

7. Advance yourself

8. Create with meaning

9. Have great people around you

10. Have fun!

"Have a Blueprint"

"Your JOURNEY, is your JOURNEY"

Worry about YOUR …
Worry about YOUR lane…
WORRY ABOUT YOURS…

TUNNEL VISION

"Navigate your roadmap to success"

NO two people have the same exact story… **WRITE YOURS**

"Remember your why…"

WORDS OF THE DAY:

IDEAS
GOALS
STRATEGIES
VISIONS
CREATIVITY
THINKING
FOCUS
PLANS
BUILDING
DREAMS
POSITIVITY

"Mindset is Everything"

DAILY REASSURANCE

If you want to be successful, you have to KILL (figuratively) something every day…

NO DAYS OFF
WIN THE DAY

ACTIONS: Help us with what we know versus what we "think"

*Without **ACTIONS** how can we reach success just watching, thinking, wondering?*

"Go out there and tell your story"

"Hard work beats talent, when talent doesn't work hard!"

HARD WORK IS THE KEY
PAY YOUR DUES

Find and **COMMIT** *to*
YOUR PURPOSE

WISDOM
FOCUS
ENERGY
EXECUTE

"Start with what you have right now...What you have is plenty" NO EXCUSES!

"If it was easy, everybody would be doing it"

FIND A MIRROR:

THE **CHALLENGE** IS YOU!

SELF AWARENESS
SELF EVALUATION
ACCOUNTABILITY
LEARNING FROM MISTAKES
STANDING 10 TOES

"All winners pay a price to win"

"What price are you willing to pay?"

SACRIFICES

"*SUCCESS* is never on discount"

"*GREATNESS* is never half off"

IT'S ALL OR NOTHING

"If you give average efforts, you'll get average results"

"YOUR DREAMS WILL NEVER GO ON SALE"

"You are the sum total of CHOICES you make…"

*"Make a path where there isn't one...**SEPARATE** yourself, so that you can **ELEVATE** yourself..."*

Elevate—*to rise, or to lift up to a HIGHER position*

Rise to a more IMPORTANT or IMPRESSIVE level...

"You don't need to be perfect, you just need to GO"

"Are you ready to Elevate"

"<u>Self-Education</u> *will make you a* ***FORTUNE...***Formal-Education *will make you a* **PORTION**"

LEARN
RESEARCH
STUDY

"What did you learn today???"

"Learn something NEW every day"

(<u>The Keys to Happiness</u>)
SELF- ESTEEM
SELF- LOVE
SELF- AWARENESS
SELF- EDUCATION

"Rich is a MINDSET, not money"

"Don't let GO!"

Don't let go of tomorrow…
Don't let go of **YOUR DREAMS**

*Think/See yourself outside of
your current situation…*

**STAY DOWN
STAY THE COURSE
VISUALIZE SUCCESS**

"Only the strong survive"

"The sun always shines again"

"Have you felt like giving up? DON'T"

PUSH THROUGH

"You gotta keep going"

REALITY
NEVER GIVE UP
MATERIALIZE

"Execute your plan"

"If you're breathing, you're winning!"

ANOTHER DAY,
ANOTHER OPPORTUNITY

"Difficult times prepare us for the level up"

HUSTLE
MOTIVATE
INSPIRE

"Sometimes we just need the
right wind to fly…"

Check the weather…
Check the wind…

You wouldn't prepare for
takeoff in a thunderstorm…

You wouldn't have success flying
a kite with no wind blowing…

*"Timing is everything… if it didn't work right
now, doesn't mean it won't work later…"*

CIRCUMSTANCES

"If something doesn't work, it's okay to try
something else…or try it a different way"

*"Tell your STORY… You are **BRAVER** than you believe. **STRONGER** than you seem. You have more **GRIT** than you give yourself credit for… YOU ARE **UNSTOPPABLE**"*

*PAIN is temporary… However, quitting lasts **FOREVER***

"Is temporary pain worth quitting?"

"Don't DECREASE the goal, INCREASE the effort!"

*"To **WIN**, you have to LOSE...
To be **SUCCESSFUL**, you have to
have UNSUCCESSFUL moments...
To be **HAPPY**, you have to have
DISAPPOINTMENT..."*

MENTALITY
PREPARATION
MENTALLY PREPARED

*"Nothing worth having,
comes EASY…"*

*A wall is built ONE BRICK at a
time…*

*GOALS are achieved ONE STEP at
a time…*

*Stop looking at your **GOALS** and
DREAMS as unrealistic or unattainable...*

NOTHING HAPPENS OVERNIGHT

"If you never try, you'll never know"

"TRY AGAIN, FAIL AGAIN, FAIL BETTER"

Learn from your experiences…

STOP trying to skip the **STRUGGLE…** **STRUGGLE** *is where character is built…*

EMBRACE IT
LEARN FROM IT
GROW FROM IT

"Go with the choice that scares you the most… that's the one that helps you GROW"

MARATHON
NO RUSH

Make **SMART** *financial goals...*

S—specific
M—measurable
A—actionable
R—realistic
T—time-related

"Write down your goals"

"Check off your goals"

WEALTH
WEALTHY

"What does wealth mean to you? We all have our own definitions of how we determine wealth"

_____

_____

_____

_____

DETERMINATION
DISCIPLINE
DRIVE
DEDICATION

Keep your MIND SHARP...

Keep a WINNER'S mentality...

NO EXCUSES

"You can CRY, or you can FLY"

"Only thing stopping you, is YOU"

"You gotta go THROUGH it, to get TO IT…"

Have a different level of **DRIVE**

"The more you sweat in practice, the less you bleed in battle"

PUT THE WORK IN
MAKE A WAY
HANDLE YOUR BUSINESS

"Look challenges in the face"

NEVER TAKE A LOSS & FEEL DEFEATED

"LEARN FROM IT"

"Come back STRONGER"

*"Become a **WELL-OILED** machine"*

ROUTINE
ROUTINE
ROUTINE

*"A sequence of **ACTIONS** regularly followed"*

GOOD HABITS
GREAT HABITS
SELF-DISCIPLINE

Patience= Core to Success

BLOOD
SWEAT
TEARS

"Level of Separation"

"Everything negative- pressure, challenges, etc.- it's all a chance to **RISE TO THE OCCASION** "

SACRIFICES
CONFIDENCE
PREPARATION

BUILD MUSCLE MEMORY

MAMBA MENTALITY
TRAIN YOUR MIND
    PASSION
    DRIVE
    WANT TO

"What drives you???"

_____

_____

_____

_____

"Educate yourself...APPLY the information..."

WORDS OF THE DAY:

GROW
PROCESS
PROGRESS
JOURNEY
MARATHON

"Knowledge is POWER"

ATTITUDE
WORK-ETHIC
EXECUTION
REPETITION

"Whether you THINK you can, or can't, you're right!"

(Let that statement above sink in)

DISCIPLINE
ENERGY
CONSISTENCY

NEVER GIVE UP ON YOURSELF

LEAD...
LEADER...
LEADERSHIP...

Extraordinary= I CAN
Average= I CAN'T

EYESIGHT VS. MINDSIGHT

PERCEPTION

What is vs. What will be...

FIND A SOLUTION

BE SMART
BE RESILIENT

A Man is a **GREAT LEADER**

Sacrifice now= WIN LATER

THINK LONG-TERM

"Are you worried about the now, or the later?"

"No work= No results"

WORK

"How can you be upset, or place blame, when you know you didn't put the work in?"

DO WHATEVER IT TAKES

BE HONEST WITH YOURSELF
ACCEPT YOUR FLAWS
WORK ON YOUR FLAWS

WORK HARDER
MAKE ADJUSTMENTS
DO BETTER!
BE BETTER!

"What are a few things you could work on to improve yourself?

*"Only those who will **RISK**
going too far, can find out
how far one can go…"*

See how far you can take yourself…

*See what you can accomplish if you
really buckle down and focus in...*

PUSH YOUR LIMITS
TEST YOUR LIMITS

"You'll never know, if you never try"

"Don't think about it, just do it"

*"What's something you've been wanting to do, but
haven't taken action quite yet?"*

_____

_____

_____

_____

_____

_____

_____

"Never settling but setting every **GOAL** *high. One thousand burpees on my* **PATH TO SUCCESS**… *but what's a mistake without the* **LESSON**? *See, the best teacher in* **LIFE** *is your own experiences… None of us know who we are until we fail"*

"Who would you want to **DEFINE** *you? Someone else, or YOURSELF?"*

HEART
STRENGTH
BELIEF

3 STEPS IN BECOMING
SUCCESSFUL:

1.   Eliminate anything NEGATIVE—toxic people/ places/ things

2.   Surround yourself with POSITIVITY—people/ places/ things

3.   BELIEVE IN YOURSELF

NEVER GIVE UP

"You can lose 99 times, but all it takes is 1 win to change your life"

"Don't stop and be upset when you realize you were almost at the finish line"

"WHAT STORY WILL YOU TELL?"

There's always tomorrow, only lasts so long...

In 15 years, when you are sitting back reflecting on your life, what is it you want to be able to say you accomplished?

List below your dreams, aspirations, goals, etc....

_____

_____

_____

_____

_____

_____

_____

_____

_____

_____

_____

*"Don't sell yourself short. **DREAM BIG**"*

*"In the midst of every OBSTACLE,
is an OPPORTUNITY"*

AWARENESS
*"Look at every obstacle
as an opportunity"*

MINDSET
POINT OF VIEW
ADJUST YOUR THINKING

"Blessings in Disguise"

"Can you pass the tests life throws at you?

STRATEGY
EXECUTE
HAVE A PLAN

WORD OF THE DAY:

FUNDAMENTALS

- The basics
- The essentials
- You have to have these FIRST

ONE PERSON...
ONE IDEA...
ONE ACTION...

SHORT- TERM L's

LONG- TERM W's

SEE THE BIGGER PICTURE...

"Are you perfecting the fundamentals of your craft?"

"The **PAST** is where you learned the lesson. The **FUTURE** is where you apply the lesson"

Don't give up in the middle...

LESSONS= BLESSINGS

"What lessons have you learned along your journey to success?"

_____

_____

_____

_____

_____

_____

_____

_____

"WHAT'S ON MY MIND..."

ELEVATE, THEN CELEBRATE

KNOW YOUR ROLE, PLAY IT WELL

DON'T TALK ABOUT IT, BE ABOUT IT

CONTROL YOUR EMOTIONS

MENTALITY

WINNERS WIN

CONTROL WHAT YOU CAN CONTROL

DO WHATEVER IT TAKES

"What's on your mind today?"

_____

_____

_____

_____

_____

"Look at yourself from the outside, looking in"

*"Mistakes are a fact of life. It's the **response** to error, that counts..."*

Don't be afraid to fail…
Don't be afraid to take risks…
Don't be afraid to take a loss…

"It's all a part of the game"

MINOR SETBACKS, MAJOR COMEBACKS

"Struggles are required in order to survive in life, because in order to **STAND UP** you have to know what **FALLING DOWN** feels like…"

"5 THINGS TO QUIT"

1. Trying to please everyone

2. Fearing change

3. Living in the past

4. Putting yourself down

5. OVERTHINKING

"If you don't believe in yourself, why should anybody else?"

WAKE UP

"If you can't solve easy problems now, you won't be able to solve difficult problems later"

"VOTE FOR YOURSELF"

Vote to put **YOURSELF** *in a position of* **POWER**…

Take **CONTROL** *of your own life*…

You are the **PRESIDENT**

"Your MIND & HEART need to start being the campaign manager of your life"

DOUBLE DOWN

BET ON YOURSELF

LIVE WITH THE RESULTS

"Don't just hope it's going to be alright, MAKE IT BE ALRIGHT!"

BE A PROBLEM SOLVER

BRING SOLUTIONS

"Nobody sends for a problem; they send for answers"

"You are not stuck where you are
UNLESS YOU *decide to be…"*

You are the ONLY one who can hold YOURSELF
accountable for YOUR decisions…

If something needs to **CHANGE***,*
it's up to YOU to make the
CHANGE*… (Or don't complain)*

"This life is 100% up to you…be the
change you want to see…"

ADAPT
ADJUST
ACHIEVE
ACCOMPLISH

"Trust your process"

*"An interesting thing about __**SUCCESS**__ is that it's like a breath of fresh air… although your LAST breath of air is important, it's not nearly as important as the NEXT ONE…"*

BE A HUNTER
BE A WOLF
BE A SHARK

EAT!

PATIENCE IS KEY...

FALL IN LOVE WITH PATIENCE

"People lose because they want things FAST... when life is a LONG process"

BET ON YOURSELF

"Bigger the STRUGGLE, Bigger the BLESSING"

*"We hurt ourselves because we **OBSESS** about the end of our **JOURNEY**. Focus on staying in the moment, on being **GRATEFUL** for where you are today"*

FOCUS ON YOUR SHOW

STOP WATCHING EVERYBODY ELSE'S

FOCUS ON YOU AND YOURS

TUNNEL VISION

"Put on blinders…"

"It's easy to blame somebody else"

LOOK IN THE MIRROR
BLAME YOURSELF
TAKE ACCOUNTABILITY

CORRECT YOUR ACTIONS

"Stay hungry…"

"Be your own biggest supporter"

SINK OR SWIM

"LESS TALK, MORE ACTION"

*"A simple reminder that a **VISION** without **ACTION**, is merely a **DREAM**"*

"Success does not come from what you do occasionally, but what you do **CONSISTENTLY**"

VISION
ACTIONS
SUCCESS

*"Believe BIG. The size of your **SUCCESS** is determined by the size of your **BELIEF**. Think of little goals and expect achievements. **THINK BIG GOALS** and win BIG SUCCESS"*

P DIDDY'S 10 RULES OF SUCCESS:

1. Have a champion's mindset

2. Be competitive

3. Know your self worth

4. Do what you love

5. Be serious about your DREAMS

6. Create with authenticity

7. HUSTLE, HUSTLE, HUSTLE

8. Surround yourself with greatness

9. Be super fearless

10. HAVE FUN

"Whatever I want I have to get!"

*"Don't stress about how to have a successful year... Instead, **FOCUS** on how you can **OPTIMIZE** your schedule and your **HABITS** to have a **SUCCESSFUL WEEK**..."*

THEN REPEAT THAT 52 TIMES

"If you stick to having successful weeks individually, the successful year will take care of itself"

STOP COMPLAINING

"As you're taking your next breath, someone is taking their last..."

APPRECIATE LIFE

*"When things go wrong,
don't go with it"*

You ALWAYS have a choice...

*Nobody is responsible for
your success, but YOU*

Find the **STRENGTH** TO <u>OVERCOME</u>...

Find the **STRENGTH** to <u>WORK</u>...

Find the **STRENGTH** to be <u>UNSTOPPABLE</u>...

"Use your time wisely"

DO MORE

DON'T GET LAZY

DON'T LIMIT YOURSELF

"WORK-ETHIC is the one thing you can control"

"Layer REAL patience AKA, knowing it will take a LONG-TIME, or longer than you may want, and you have a main piece of the winning formula"

*"Mold your **MINDSET** to ONLY think **POSITIVES**. ONLY think **SOLUTIONS**"*

THE CIRCLE OF WINNING:

"Ideas are worthless without execution"

"Execution is pointless without ideas"

"Success is like an iceberg..."
WHAT THEY SEE:

SUCCESS
MONEY
GLORY
REWARDS
MATERIAL ITEMS

WHAT THEY DON'T SEE:

GRIND
FAILURE
HARD-WORK
STRUGGLE
SACRIFICE
LONG NIGHTS
EARLY MORNINGS

"Are you prepared to do what it takes to be Successful?"

*"Life has so many chapters…
One bad chapter doesn't mean
it's the end of the book"*

Things to be thankful for:

LIFE
OPPORTUNITY
FAMILY
HEALTH
LOYALTY
RESPECT
#1 THE MAN ABOVE

"Anyone who has love for me, I have love for them"

"What are you thankful for?"

_____

_____

_____

_____

_____

_____

_____

_____

MAIN GOAL

LEVEL UP/ ELEVATION

"STAY IN YOUR LANE"

"STAY DOWN, UNTIL YOU COME UP"

"BE BETTER THAN YOU WERE YESTERDAY"

"YOUR ONLY COMPETITION IS YOURSELF"

FACTS> OPINIONS
SOLUTIONS> PROBLEMS
LOGIC> EMOTIONS

YOU ARE IN CONTROL

You're **BETTER** than what you're doing…

You're **BETTER** than you think...

FOCUS ON THE MISSION...

"What is your mission?"

_____

_____

_____

_____

_____

"Fall in love with losing, then you will no longer be scared…"

Are you afraid of FAILURE? Why, or why not?

_____

_____

_____

_____

_____

_____

_____

_____

"When you live for YOU, you aren't worried about losing/failure, because TRYING is the win"

TRYING > FAILING

"You win some, you lose some"

JOURNEY

TRIALS & TRIBULATIONS

Write your own story...
You are the author of your life...

GET STRONGER

PHYSICALLY
MENTALLY
SPIRITUALLY
EMOTIONALLY

The HAVES focus on the mission...
Don't be a HAVE NOT

MINDSET

LAW OF ATTRACTION

"The ability to ATTRACT into our lives what-
ever we are FOCUSING ON"

POWER OF THE MIND...

ABUNDANCE
THOUGHTS
VALUES
EMOTIONS
AWARENESS
MORALS

"If you have GOALS, aim to achieve them...you will find a way..."

FOCUS
POSITIVE THOUGHTS
ACTIONS
PLAN

MEDITATION

High frequencies...

10-15 minutes daily...

PEACE OF MIND
CONCENTRATION
VISUALIZATION
AWARENESS
CALMNESS
FOCUS
RELAXATION
TOTAL CONTROL
DEEP BREATHS

"Mental, physical, & emotional control"

"What you say, think, & do all matter"

GATHER YOUR THOUGHTS...
FREE YOUR MIND...

*"Slow success builds **character**…*
Quick success builds ego…"

"Slow and steady wins the race"

PATIENCE
DEDICATION
HARD-WORK

RESPECT THE HUSTLE…
RESPECT THE GAME…

.

MARATHON MENTALITY

"Put yourself in the driver's seat of YOUR LIFE..."

BLOOM
INCUBATE
EVOLVE
CLARITY
ENERGY
FOCUS
BALANCE
EXPLORE
CREATIVITY
IDENTIFY
PRIORITIES

*"The BIGGEST asset in the world is **YOUR MINDSET**"*

How you "SEE IT" and how you "THINK IT" is your life...

PERSPECTIVE

"Champions keep going..."

FIND A WAY, OUT OF NO WAY
MAKE A WAY

NO EXCUSES

"*What you do is 100x more IMPORTANT than what you say*"

Don't talk about it, BE ABOUT IT…

"*The number one reason people don't get what they want in LIFE, is because they QUIT or STOP*"

ADJUST
PIVOT
MODIFY

"Did you go the extra mile?"

How to get started:

- Get in alignment
- Take action
- Prepare for adjustment

Get in alignment= proper positioning. "Putting everything in order"

Action= Implement the plan

Adjustment= Expect the unexpected. STAY READY

OUR THOUGHTS

=

OUR EMOTIONS

=

OUR ACTIONS

=

OUR RESULTS

*"When you **CHANGE** your thoughts, you'll **CHANGE** your life…"*

"It's not easy, but remember, it's not supposed to be…"

Try…
Try again…
Try once more…
Try differently…
Try again tomorrow…
Try and ask for help…
Try to fix the problem…
Try and find someone who
has done it…

KEEP TRYING

FINANCIAL:

- Education
- Literacy
- Stability
- Discipline
- Independence
- FREEDOM

WEALTH…
WEALTHY…

"Build your portfolio"

"Diversify your portfolio"

"Cash/ Credit/ Save/ Invest/ Win"

WORDS OF THE DAY:

HUSTLE
LEARN
STUDY
RESOURCES
ADAPT
EDUCATE
TOOLS
RESEARCH

*"Apply your **KNOWLEDGE**
& **INFORMATION**"*

"Knowing is ½ the battle… the other ½ is DOING!"

MAN UP!

"Face your FEARS head on"

At some point, we have to be
TESTED

"Will you pass, or fail your test?"

Difficult means:

- I CAN, I WILL
- GRIT
- KEEP PUSHING
- DON'T STOP

"Fear is not real"

*"Would you rather be at **WAR** with yourself and at peace with the world, or at **PEACE** with yourself and war with the world?*

"I CAN AND I WILL"

Powerful words that should never be underestimated...

"Say these words to yourself daily..."

YOU CAN

YOU WILL

"NOTHING CAN STOP ME"

Take the first step...
Start small and build...

"Focus on the first step and not the staircase..."

Life Lessons…

99 NO's
1 YES

One life
No RE DO's
NO RESET BUTTON

ACT → ACTIONS

"Turn L's to W's"

"Tell yourself you are a winner, every day"

"Have you told yourself YOU'RE A WINNER today?"

WORD OF THE DAY:

VALUE

- "The regard that something is held to deserve; the importance, worth, or usefulness of something…"
- "A person's principles or standards of behavior; one's judgment of what is important in life…"

Find **VALUE**…
Provide **VALUE**…

"What makes you valuable?"

_____

_____

_____

_____

_____

_____

_____

WORD OF THE DAY:

PROGRESS

"Forward or onward movement toward a destination…"

"Move forward or onward in space or time…"

*"Slow progress is better than **NO** progress"*

IMPROVEMENT
DEVELOPMENT
ADVANCEMENT
GROWTH

"Are you progressing toward your GOALS/DREAMS?"

"Learn, allow yourself time to GROW…"

"Water your seeds…"

JOURNEY

"Roadblocks, Obstacles, Setbacks, Stop Signs, Turns, etc.… are ALL designed to keep you DOWN & BEHIND… take them ALL head on"

"Never stop moving forward and educating yourself"

"The ONLY true way to FAIL, is to QUIT"

"For every MISTAKE, every ACTION, every bit of SUCCESS, it's the beauty of the **JOURNEY**"

*"Enjoy the pursuit of reaching your full **POTENTIAL**"*

Realize your potential…

"Having, or showing the capability to become, or develop into something"

"Qualities, or abilities that may be developed and lead to future success"

INSPIRATION

BE INSPIRED

"Be prepared for the opportunity you have been waiting for…"

"Stay ready so you don't have to get ready…"

*PROPER
PREPARATION
PREVENTS
POOR
PERFORMANCE*

"It's **YOU** vs **YOU**, EVERYDAY…"

"The faster you understand the **TRUE BATTLE** is within and we have **NO ONE** to blame, but ourselves… The faster you can progress toward your **GOALS**"

"Comparisons will rob you from joy… Learn from others, but don't compare… Your time will come…"

"Are you winning the battle of you vs. you?

WRITE YOUR OWN BOOK
TELL YOUR OWN STORY
BE THE AUTHOR
OF YOUR LIFE…

"PRESSURE MAKES DIAMONDS"

*"Your **LONG-TERM** success
is a byproduct of your
CONDITIONING..."*

NO STRUGGLE
NO STRENGTH

SUCCESS:

HAPPINESS
PATIENCE
HARD-WORK

"Open up your MIND…"

*GET OUT YOUR
COMFORT ZONE*

PLANT & SPREAD YOUR SEEDS…

*GROWTH
DEVELOP
PATIENCE*

**NO
RUSH**

"What seeds are you planting?"

_____

_____

_____

_____

_____

*"Maximize the time you have and make the necessary **SACRIFICES** to win…"*

WORD OF THE DAY:

DISCIPLINE

- Control gained by enforcing obedience, or order
- Orderly, or prescribed conduct, or pattern of behavior
- SELF CONTROL

*"**DISCIPLINE** will take you to places where **MOTIVATION** can't…"*

"When motivation runs out, let discipline take its place…"

"If you want to become SUCCESSFUL, you have to take 100% responsibility for everything you experience in YOUR LIFE…"

"We are not always liable, but we are ACCOUNTABLE…"

"What am I supposed to learn from this?"

"Every mistake is a MIRICLE, if we learn from it…"

"It's not just about what you **LEARN**... *it's about being aware enough to* **APPLY** *what you've* **LEARNED** *when it's time..."*

"Success doesn't just land in your lap"

WORK
WORK
WORK

"Believe it, then achieve it"

IT ALL STARTS WITH YOU

"You can't cheat the game.
You can't cheat the grind."

"Stop focusing on what you
DON'T HAVE *and start focusing*
on what you **DO HAVE"**

NO HANDOUTS
NO COMPLAINTS

NOTHING IS FREE

"The moment you give up, the moment you let somebody else win…"

"Are you grateful for what you have thus far in life?"

"The struggle is temporary"

"Sacrifices are like investments…
give up short-term comfort,
for long-term wins"

Stay patient…
Stay focused…
Stay dedicated…
Stay the course…

"You can't be AVERAGE and be a LEGEND"

BE LEGENDARY

OKAY
GOOD
GREAT
EXCELLENT
PHENOMINAL
LEGENDARY STATUS

"Do you have what it takes to reach legendary status?"
"What's your definition of being a LEGEND?"

_____

_____

_____

_____

_____

_____

_____

"Determine your destination…"

Where do you want to go?

_____

_____

_____

What is it going to take to get there?

_____

_____

_____

FOCUS IN
BLINDERS
END GOAL
NO DISTRACTIONS

"Are you ready?
"Are you prepared"

"You can't cut corners"

"You have to EARN it"

"Always take ADVANTAGE"

"Position yourself"

"BE GREAT"

"Start telling yourself you're WORTHY of all things it is you want…then put the work in to get it"

READY,
SET,
GO

"Your NETWORK, is your NETWORTH!"

Build relationships

CONNECTIONS
IRON SHARPENS IRON
RUB SHOULDERS

HANG AROUND THOSE YOU
WANT TO LEARN FROM
LEARN FROM EACHOTHER

LEARN SOMETHING
NEW EVERYDAY
TEACH SOMETHING
NEW EVERYDAY

"PURSUIT OF HAPPINESS"

Stay true to your CODE
Stay true to your BELIEFS
Stay true to YOU

"Always work on becoming a better YOU and a better person"

"What is your definition of happiness?"

_____

_____

_____

_____

_____

"What brings happiness to your life?"

_____

_____

_____

_____

_____

*"Going into every new day,
new month, new year…"*

Higher frequencies…
Higher vibrations…

NEW WAVELENGTHS

Manifest
Manifestation
ELEVATION

*"You owe it to yourself to be the
BEST YOU, you can be…"*

ALWAYS KEEP IMPROVING

"Keep planting your seeds…"

"MAMBA MENTALITY"

"Always keep going..."

"The storm eventually ends..."

"If you're going to do something, do it
to the best of your ability..."

"Create and inspire..."

"Consume yourself with the quest of
trying to be the best..."

"Always ask questions..."

"Definition of greatness is to inspire
the people next to you..."

*"Don't chase money, chase **accomplishments**"*

*"Don't chase money, chase your **dreams**"*

*"Don't chase money, chase your **passion**"*

"Far too often we think about the money, not realizing when you chase the 3 quotes above, that's all the satisfaction we need. Everything else will fall into place…"

"Money will be around… they print new bills every day! Most importantly, we can't take it with us. What we can take with us is each and every day, we chased our accomplishments, dreams, & Passions…."

"Money will come…"

Habakkuk 2:2

*"Write the **VISION** and make it plain, so that HE who reads it, WILL RUN TO IT"*

"Wait for it, for SURELY it will come at an appointed time…"

WRITE IT DOWN

MAP OUT YOUR VISION BOARD

"You have not cus' you ask not…"

My daily prayer:

Simple…

*I pray for 3 things every
morning when I wake up
and before I go to sleep…*

DIRECTION

GUIDANCE

OPPORTUNITY

"What is it you pray for?"

_____

_____

_____

_____

"Key takeaways"

_____

_____

_____

_____

_____

_____

_____

_____

_____

_____

_____

_____

_____

_____

_____

_____

_____

_____

_____

_____

_____

_____

"Speak your mind…"

"Express Yourself..."

"Creative canvas"

"Creative canvas"

_____

_____

_____

_____

_____

_____

_____

_____

_____

_____

_____

_____

_____

_____

_____

_____

_____

_____

_____

"Creative canvas"

Bucket List Page:

It's important for all of us to have an active bucket list of achievements/ goals/ destinations/ etc. so that we have a clear understanding of what we want in life. Actively engage with your "*bucket list*" and do whatever it takes to cross every item listed below: "This is what we live for"

_____

_____

_____

_____

_____

_____

_____

_____

_____

_____

_____

_____

_____

_____

_____

_____

_____

Special S/O page:

I would like to list the various individuals below whose wise words had an influence and impact toward creating the content within this journal.

"Be a student of the game…"

- Nipsey Hussle
- Rick Ross
- Dame Dash
- Master P
- Jay Z
- P Diddy
- EYL (Earn Your Leisure)
- Million Dollars' Worth of Game
- Wallo267
- GaryVee
- Warren Buffet
- T.D Jakes
- Steve Harvey
- Eric Thomas (Motivational Speaker)
- Daymond John (Fubu/ Shark Tank)
- Prince Donnel
- And many more …

"About the author"

Shawn Rogers was born in Des Moines, IA. He currently lives in Atlanta, GA and always had a strong writing background. From storytelling, personal poems, and journaling, he wanted to finally take that next step and get something professionally published.

A college graduate from the University of Iowa and employee within the corporate world, he has experienced the ups and downs of what comes with being someone approaching their 30th birthday. The feeling of not being as accomplished as he wished he would be years and years ago, but with maturity, realizing he is just getting started.

We look at reaching 30 years of age, as being "old" when we're in our mid to late teens and early 20s, so we apply unnecessary pressure on ourselves feeling we need to have this, or already accomplished that to classify ourselves successful. That is far from the case.

Someone in my shoes, living everyday life, seeing our peers reach a certain level of success either before, or after us, is how we measure our own success. It takes time and maturity to realize we are only in competition with ourselves. We are in a race with no one. As long as we're progressing and maximizing each day to the best of our abilities, setting goals and achieving them, we are on the road to success.

Still trying to figure out his mission and passion in life, writing is an outlet of expression. Setting goals and continuing to write out his daily thoughts, his main pursuit is finding what really drives him. What does he see himself doing the next 5-10 years? Next 15-20? This is the best part of not being in a rush, taking things as they come. It's all a part of his journey. The best is yet to come.

CPSIA information can be obtained
at www.ICGtesting.com
Printed in the USA
BVHW090906150222
629067BV00003B/262